THE PERSEUS SERIES

Sir Edward Coley Burne-Jones

Southampton | City Art Gallery

Sir Edward Coley Burne-Jones in his studio (1898)
by Philip Burne-Jones
Courtesy of National Portrait Gallery, London

BURNE-JONES
A PAINTER
OF SOULS

It has often been said that the art of Burne-Jones was escapist, not only for the artist himself but also for his audience.[1] The realities of late 19th century life apparently drove the artist into an imaginary dream world peopled not with the living but with beautiful souls. He has also been accused of nostalgia, for trying to recapture a lost heroic past.[2] His world could be in the past, with its references to both classical myths and medieval legends but essentially it is time-less, like 'some other place of being'.[3] In his essay of 1883 John Ruskin recognised Burne-Jones as a painter of mythology and personification, his symbolic figures representing 'only general truths or abstract ideas'.[4] Burne-Jones' works appealed to the intellectual elite of the Victorian world. He chose an imaginary mythical world in order to explore the meaning and purpose of life. You did not go to Burne-Jones for naturalism or realism. Many of his very successful contemporaries like William Powell Frith, Sir Luke Fildes and Jacques Joseph Tissot painted scenes of modern life, or social-realist subjects, recording both the mannerisms and extremes in dress of later Victorian society.[5] Instead Burne-Jones chose a high, elevated style that portrays a noble humanity. He considered modern life to be ugly and sought an alternative world in which beauty ruled supreme. Of course his world is not easy for us to understand. At first sight it is rather rarified and precious, remote and even irrelevant to our lives but many of us share the same concerns about modern society as the artist, that a lack of beauty will dehumanise and brutalise us. His works require us to think, they are not instantly comprehended. The images are deliberately ambiguous, with much of the interpretation left to the viewer. It is this that makes his images so intriguing, while his uncertainty shows a human side which endears him to his audience. Unlike George Frederick Watts, who also used a mythic world in which to explore man's experiences, Burne-Jones achieved a popular appeal which he has maintained to this day. As Henry James noted, 'His expression is complicated, troubled; but at least there is an interesting mind in it'.[6]

His images are troubling. His androgynous male and female figures may have been an attempt to arrive at a form of genetic perfection, akin to an angel but for some their sexuality is disturbing. Even his knights in shining armour and damsels in distress seem to suffer from 'ennui', a sort of bored indifference, even when faced with the immediate plight of being eaten by a seamonster. On occasions Burne-Jones' view is fatalistic, born out of his own obsession with the 'hand of fate' and fortune. He was fascinated by certain grand themes, the sacred and profane, love and loss, sacrifice and reward, fulfilment and redemption, birth and death, good and evil, order and chaos, all the core subjects of myths from the earliest times of human history. At a time when technical reason and scientific investigation called into question the mystical and the spiritual, Burne-Jones transports us into a primordial paradise, where man faces for the first time the natural cycle of life, in which life flows out of death. The barren landscapes of *The Perseus Series* do not distract from the significant action, the eternal struggle of good and evil. Only the final panel, the *Baleful Head* (illustrated p. 39) presents a true Garden of Eden, in which our hero is triumphant and duly rewarded. Burne-Jones' images can be likened to a mirror or a lens through which we peer into an alternative world. Like Lewis Carroll he takes us through the looking glass.[7] It seems that we are happy to accept this world in which the impossible can happen, a world inhabited with monsters, creatures half-human and half-beast, with gods and goddesses and with heroes and heroines. Burne-Jones uses a visual language, based on poetry and religion, that 'draws on image, metaphor and narrative in such a way that it evokes ideas, feelings and intuitions in an encompassing way'.[8] By his use of this language Burne-Jones embodies ideas, he gives us insight into a world of darkness and light, corruption and renewal, of death and birth. He allows us to confront our worst fears and yet he always gives us hope. He gives us something high to aim for, goals that could be achieved but only through diligence and hard work, a kind of dogged determination to rise above the mundane and ordinary, the perpetual rush of life, to the transcendental.

Above all Burne-Jones presents a world in which spiritual values are paramount. Perhaps this was Burne-Jones' personal response to modern life, for the later 19th century witnessed, as one of the consequences of the Aesthetic movement, the commodification of art itself, that last and greatest bastion of the spiritual. The democratisation or vulgarisation of the arts had resulted in mass consumerism. Art was reduced to yet another commodity, to be bought and sold and generally exploited. Its acquisition was required for social enhancement: art philanthropy, patronage and collecting gave the leisured or 'unoccupied classes something to do at a time when they needed to 'earn their salt in a busy world'.[9] For the aspiring classes art was a useful tool for stepping up into the higher orders. At all levels of society, art was seen as educationally enriching and improving, it assumed a moral dimension and was generally seen as a force for good within the community.[10]

Burne-Jones was linked, through his relationship with both John Ruskin and William Morris, to this notion of art, or beauty, as a force for good, 'the love of which empowers us to do and be good'. By 1900 his art had been linked to a certain brand of Englishness which embraced medievalism and chivalry and was exemplified in the pseudo-Elizabethan mansion which was created by Sir Edwin Lutyens to house the Morris and Co. exhibit at the Paris Universal Exposition. With its preoccupation with Arthurian legends and the Quest for the Holy Grail, his art became associated with establishment values: duty, honour and courage. These values would be hard pressed with the onslaught of the First World War.

However, the artist's own attitude to the moral purpose of art was far from certain. The viewer's response to his complex and contradictory images was to be entirely personal. Burne-Jones was not concerned with allegory, something universally understood and devoid of all mystery but as he tells us himself with 'suggestions'.[11] His figures are 'types', which perhaps accounts for the androgynous character of his men and women. Both are equally beautiful in body and spirit. The Burne-Jones type is instantaneously recognisable: his women, normally virginal girls or maidens, are thin, waif-like, with pale complexions, large 'soulful' eyes and mournful expressions. They have an abundance of hair but none of the sensuality of Dante Gabriel Rossetti's Venetian-style temptresses. Burne-Jones' girls glide in their diaphanous white dresses, they have an asexual romanticism but essentially they are untouchable for they are not of this world. As a painter of the soul, Burne-Jones was supreme, capturing the invisible and impalpable mysteries of life and death. In his later works he created a new type of woman who was 'aristocratic in soul or spirit',[12] based on the girls who had supported and encouraged him during the 'desolate years of the 1870s'.[13]

Inspired by Margaret, his own daugther, Frances Graham,[14] Mary Gladstone and Mary Stuart-Wortley, Burne-Jones created a commonwealth of beauty, not based on social class or blood lineage but on a personal response to art and beauty. Burne-Jones, like William Morris, believed that an 'instinct for beauty … is inborn in every complete man' and therefore, art was a 'positive necessity of life'.[15] Art was to be the great leveller, overcoming accidents of birth, fortune or education. A love of art was universal and art was, according to Morris, to be 'shared by gentle and simple, learned and unlearned, and be as a language that all can understand'.[16] Burne-Jones popularised a beauty which all could appreciate, by appealing to the imagination of the spectator as an 'endowed soul', in effect soul communing with soul.[17] Burne-Jones credits us with the rarified sensibilities of the artist himself. He professed not to mind that his works appeared next to advertisements for tooth-paste, as long as the public had access to beauty. Through a love and appreciation of art anybody can attain the same spiritual transfor-mation, can be lifted out of themselves to a higher plane. However, the notion of an aesthetic elite, 'an aristocracy of mind or spirit dwelling among the teeming masses of the modern age', was also implicit within this notion, as was recognised by Oscar Wilde.[18]

However, the Burne-Jones figure-type did not command universal appeal and the artist was often condemned for his lifeless poses, vacant expressions and melancholia: 'the lugubriousity with which E. Burne-Jones clouds every countenance, even that of Love and the Goddess Venus, he will lift someday when his philosophy is riper and healthier — when he has discovered that all mankind, especially womankind, do not walk about the world like hired mutes at a funeral'.[19] For some she was unnatural, for her self-absorption undermined her social duties as a wife and mother. A preoccupation with art had led to her bodily decline and morbidity. Her melancholia was due to her search for the unob-tainable, for spiritual transformation. William Gilbert in *Patience*, his famous satire on hyper-aesthesia, also concluded that she was a love-sick maiden but the cause of her grief had taken on manly form in the shape of the poet Bunthorne. Quite simply the *High Art Maiden* as she was popularised on the stage and in satirical cartoons by Gerard Du Maurier and Linley Sambourne was the victim of unrequited love. The French art critic Octave Mirbeau also found the Burne-Jones type easy prey:[20]

a soul is only a stake, with, here and there, a lily, an iris and a poppy … Sometimes she holds a lyre in her hand, or a frond … and her eyes are drawn and blackened … When people would explain Burne-Jones to me long ago, they would say: 'Please note the hematoma around the eyes; it is unique in art. One cannot tell whether it is occasioned by self-abuse or lesbian practices, by natural love or by tuberculosis … That is the key to everything'.

However, as Henry James noted Burne-Jones was:

not a votary of the actual … It is beside the mark to say that his young women are sick, for they are neither sick nor well. They live in a different world from ours — a fortunate world in which young ladies may be slim and pale and 'seedy without discredit and (I trust) without discomfort. It is not a question of sickness and health; it is a question of grace, delicacy, tenderness, of the chord of association and memory'.[21]

Burne-Jones created a type of beauty that was as recognisable as that of Botticelli or Rossetti, which defines the artist's identity rather than communicating the nature of the sitter. Perhaps this accounts for the artist's self-admitted failure as a portrait painter: 'I do not easily get portraiture — and the perpetual hunt to find in a face what I like and leave out what mislikes me, is a bad school of it'.[22] Even when he attempted portraits, 'some imperative instinct of selection deflected his hand from what he saw with his eyes to the image of his inner vision'.[23] As types his figures were bound to be 'monotonous', his compositions 'conceptions', his subjects 'unreal', the treatment 'artifical' and the intention 'obscure' but, 'If his figures are too much of the same family, no English painter of our day has mastered a single type so completely and made it an image of so many different things'.[24]

ANNE ANDERSON

NOTES AND REFERENCES

[1]   William Gaunt, *The Aesthetic Adventure*, London, 1945, pp. 93, 212.

[2]   For examples of general comments see Penelope Fitzgerald, *Edward Burne-Jones: A Biography*, London, 1975, reprinted 1997; Martin Harrison and Bill Waters, *Burne-Jones*, London, 1973; John Dixon Hunt, *The Pre-Raphaelite Imagination 1848-1900*, London, 1968; David Cecil, *Visionary and Dreamer: Two Poetic Painters — Samuel Palmer and Edward Burne-Jones*, London, 1969; Frances Spalding, *Magnificent Dreams: Burne-Jones and the late Victorians*, Oxford, 1978.

[3]   Geoffrey Galt Harpham, *On the Grotesque: Strategies of Contradiction in Art and Literature*, Princeton, N.J., 1982, p. 43.

[4]   John Ruskin, *The Art of England: Lecture 2 — Mythic Schools of Painting — Burne-Jones and G.F. Watts*, 1883, reprinted London, 1898, pp. 55-56. G.F. Watts, who greatly influenced the younger Burne-Jones during the 1860s, also used myths and legends to explore human experience and values.

[5]   J.J. Tissot's *The Captain's Daughter*, in the Southampton City Art Gallery Collection, provides a good example of this type of painting, characterised by John Ruskin as merely tinted photographs.

[6]   quoted from J. L. Sweeney, *The Painter's Eye: notes and essays on the pictorial arts by Henry James*, London, 1956, p. 205.

[7]   Burne-Jones' fixation with reflective surfaces is amply illustrated in *The Call of Perseus* and *The Baleful Head*. In the latter he employs the unbroken surface of the water to visualise the alter-ego of Woman, the reflected image revealing the darker side of human nature.

[8]   Ernst Cassirer, *Language and Myth*, trans. Susanne K. Langer, New York, 1946, Chapter 3, quoted from James Luther Adams and Wilson Yates, *The Grotesque in Art and Literature: Theological Reflections*, Grand Rapids, Michigan/Cambridge, 1997, p. 42.

[9]   Edith Simox, 'Ideals of Feminine Usefulness', *Fortnightly Review*, 1880, pp. 656-71. The upper classes were required to 'work' as a moral duty. Ladies with time on their hands turned to art philan-

thropy. Amateur exhibitions and bazaars allowed works to be shown and the proceeds were usually donated to a good cause. Artistic practice and exhibition in the public sphere thereby fulfilled the need to 'do good works'. This precipitated the art boom of the 1870s and 1880s, in which a glut of amateur art work threatened the professional artist.

[10]   Ruskin and Morris both promoted a 'moral aestheticism' which perceived art as a means of improving Victorian society. Morris was particularly concerned with modes of production, the value of the worker within society and with communal responsibility. See Linda Dowling, *The Vulgarisation of Art: the Victorians and Aesthetic Democracy*, University Press of Virginia, 1996.

[11]   'in fact you only want types, symbols, suggestions', quoted from A.W. Baldwin, *The Macdonald Sisters*, London, 1960, pp. 142-43.

[12]   Linda Dowling, *The Vulgarisation of Art: the Victorians and Aesthetic Democracy*, University Press of Virginia, 1996, p. xii. See for example *The Golden Stairs* and *King Cophetua and the Beggar Maid* both in the Tate Gallery, London.

[13]   During this decade Burne-Jones declined to exhibit and he became rather isolated. He relied on the patronage of his closest friends and admirers. He did not resume exhibiting until 1877, with the opening of the Grosvenor Gallery. His deliberate retreat from the world may have been precipitated by his disastrous love-affair with the Greek beauty, Maria Zambaco.

[14]   The profile of Frances Graham, later Lady Horner, can be seen in *The Call of Perseus*. For Burne-Jones she was the Soul's Beauty.

[15]   Linda Dowling, *The Vulgarisation of Art: the Victorians and Aesthetic Democracy*, University Press of Virginia, 1996, p. 51, quoting from Morris (Works, 23:168).

[16]   Ibid., p. 50, quoting Morris (Works, 22:165).

[17]   As expressed by Baudelaire, 'The principal source of interest (of the work of art) derives from the soul (of the artist) and irresistibly reaches the soul of the onlooker', quoted from Henri

Dorra, *Symbolist Art Theories: A Critical Anthology*, Berkeley, 1994, p. 6.

[18]   Ibid., pp. 96-97.

[19]   *The Art Journal*, 1878, p. 155.

[20]   Octave Mirbeau, 'Les Artistes de l'âme, *Le Journal*, Feb 23, 1896, quoted from Henri Dorra, *Symbolist Art Theories: A Critical Anthology*, Berkeley, 1994, p. 278.

[21]   J.L. Sweeney, *The Painter's Eye: notes and essays on the pictorial arts by Henry James*, London, 1956, p. 206.

[22]   A.W. Baldwin, *The Macdonald Sisters*, London, 1960, p. 142.

[23]   Cosmo Monkhouse, Introduction to *Drawings and Studies of Edward Burne-Jones*, Burlington Fine Arts Club Exhibition, London, 1899.

[24]   Ibid., p. 163.

Perseus and the Sea Nymphs (detail)

THE
PERSEUS
STORY

The Greek myths are a collection of stories invented by the ancients through
which they attempted to make sense of the world around them. It would be a
mistake to think of them in the way we think of a modern novel – as a
sequence of events composed by a single author, written down and fixed
forever. They were retold by word of mouth for hundreds of years and, while
the basic thread of the story might remain constant, details could be varied
here and there by successive narrators according to their particular interests
and contemporary circumstances. Classical poets used the stories as source
material; skeletons upon which to hang moral tales or theatrical tragedies;
and from the earliest time, visual artists have referred to them when in need
of a narrative basis for their own productions.

The Perseus legend has been one of the most popular of these heroic tales;
Aeschylus, Euripides and Ovid related it in one form or another; Charles
Kingsley, William Morris and Robert Graves are among those writers to retell
it in modern times, there is even an opera by Richard Strauss based on the
early part of the story. Its combination of excitement, violence, sensuality
and ultimate morality – all the baddies eventually get their just desserts, while
all the good guys live happily ever after – has made it attractive to almost all
periods and all persuasions. Even the early Christians – not noted for their
tolerance of the Classics – saw in the story a prefiguration of Christ's victory

over the powers of evil and the foundation of a new era. In the visual arts it has provided themes for painters as varied as Titian, Correggio and Rembrandt, though perhaps the most well-known example is the bronze sculpture in Florence by Benvenuto Cellini. This gory piece shows Perseus standing over Medusa's dead body, holding aloft the terrible head with its writhing snakes and bloody dripping neck.

The parts of the legend illustrated here by Burne-Jones are the central episodes – Perseus' search for a victory over the Gorgon Medusa, and the meeting with his bride Andromeda – but to understand fully what is going on it might be useful to look back briefly to the beginning of the story.

Perseus was born the son of Danaë and Zeus, the King of the Gods of Olympus. Acrisius, Danaë's father and King of Argos, had imprisoned his daughter in an impregnable subterranean chamber to prevent her ever having children as he had been told by the oracle at Delphi that his grandson would be the cause of his death. However, Zeus transformed himself into a golden rain and entered the chamber (presumably through the air vents) to fulfil his passion for Danaë, and in the course of time, she gave birth to a son. When he discovered the child, Acrisius had Danaë and Perseus locked into a chest and set adrift on the open sea, hoping that they would either drown or die of hunger and thirst, but they were released by a fisherman, Diktys, when the chest was washed up on the island of Seriphos in the Cyclades. Here Perseus grew peacefully into adolescence, until Polydectes, the King of Seriphos, jealous of the young man's physique, and anxious to seduce Danaë, plotted to remove him. The King gave a great banquet to which all those invited, Perseus among them, were required to bring a horse as a gift. Perseus, still living in the household of the fisherman Diktys, was too poor to bring such a grand present and Polydectes hoped this would shame him into leaving Seriphos. Instead, the young man arrived empty-handed, but demonstrated his honour by swearing to bring Polydectes whatever he desired, even if it were the head of Medusa. His choice of this gift is not as arbitrary as it may seem to us – in very ancient traditions Medusa is described as having the body of a horse, and she appears in that form on at least one archaic amphora (Athena is held responsible for this distressing condition, see p. 29), Perseus is, therefore, offering the head of the most 'unique' horse in existence, and the most dangerous since Medusa's appearance is terrifying – she has living snakes instead of hair and her stare turns mortal things to inanimate stone. Polydectes accepts the offer delightedly; the Gorgons live at the end of the earth, and if Perseus survives the hazardous journey he will almost certainly be petrified by Medusa's glance, and having made this declaration before the assembled guests at the feast, he would be too ashamed to return empty-handed. The King would be rid of him and Danaë would be defenceless. It is at this particular point that Burne-Jones' illustrations begin.

THE CHARACTERS

ACRISIUS
King of Argos, father of Danaë, grandfather of Perseus.

ANDROMEDA
Daughter of Cepheus and Cassiopeia, wife of Perseus.

ATHENA
Goddess of wisdom and war, daughter of Zeus,
patron of Perseus.

ATLAS
A Titan, condemned forever to support the sky.

CASSIOPEIA
Wife of Cepheus, mother of Andromeda, eventually
placed in the sky as a constellation.

CEPHEUS

*King of Joppa in Ethiopia, father of Andromeda,
like his wife eventually transferred to the sky as a
constellation.*

CHRYSAOR

*Son of Medusa and Poseidon, born from the blood of
Medusa's severed head.*

DANAE

*Daughter of Acrisius, seduced by Zeus,
mother of Perseus.*

DELPHIC ORACLE

*The most important oracle in Greece, whose
predictions were famous for their ambiguity.*

DIKTYS

*A fisherman, later King of Seriphos, protector of
Danaë and Perseus.*

GRAIAE

*Daughters of Phorkys, sisters of the Gorgons,
grey-haired from birth, with only one eye and
one tooth between them.*

HADES

*God of the Underworld, the land of the dead,
whose helmet made anyone wearing it invisible,
brother of Zeus.*

HERMES

*God of travellers, traders and thieves; son of Zeus
and messenger of the gods, whose winged sandals
were loaned to Perseus.*

MEDUSA
Daughter of Phorkys, the only mortal one of the three
Gorgons. She had offended Athena and had been
turned into a hideously ugly creature with snakes instead
of hair, a look so terrifying it turned people to stone
and, in some accounts, the body of a horse.

PEGASUS
A winged horse, the offspring of Medusa and Poseidon,
born from the blood of Medusa's severed head.

PHORKYS
Father of the Gorgons and the Graiae, one of the older
generation of deities before Zeus and the Olympians.

POLYDECTES
King of Seriphos, turned to stone by Perseus.

POSEIDON
God of the sea, whose emblems were the trident
and the horse. Seducer of Medusa, enemy of Athena
and brother of Zeus.

TITANS
A race of pre-Olympian Gods, frequently
referred to as giants.

ZEUS
King of the Gods of Mount Olympus, seducer of Danaë,
father of Athena, Hermes and Perseus.

1

THE CALL OF PERSEUS

Perseus sits on the bank of a stream outside the city, naked and dejected, already regretting his impetuosity. A heavily draped figure stands over him, sympathetically holding out a hand. This is the goddess Athena who reveals herself to Perseus' startled eyes in the centre of the picture, wearing the armour traditionally associated with her (she is the goddess of wisdom, and secondarily, of war, and is said to have emerged fully armed from the head of her father Zeus). Athena has overheard the conversation at the feast, and her hatred of the Gorgons (daughters of the ancient deity Phorkys) is such that she comes to Perseus' aid. She advises him about his journey, warns him of Medusa's stony stare, and, traditionally, she lends him a highly polished shield in which he will be able to see Medusa's reflection without risking the dreadful consequences of looking at her directly. (in the painting this shield has become a mirror — conveniently small and portable, and just as effective).

It is interesting to see how Burne-Jones makes use of an old-fashioned pictorial device to assist his narrative. On the one hand he is limited by the commission to ten panels, on the other he feels the need to refer to both the incidents depicted here, and so he includes both episodes in the same picture space, allowing the characters to appear twice in the same continuous landscape.

2

PERSEUS AND THE GRAIAE

Athena belongs to the younger generation of Greek deities, the siblings and
children of Zeus. Older than this set, and more deeply rooted in the
subconscious of the Greeks and other European ethnic groups are deities
whose roles and powers are less clearly defined, but whom the Olympian gods
never completely supplanted. The Gorgons and their sisters the Graiae are
among them. The Graiae lived in a land of darkness, near the ends of the
earth, as near to the east as it is to the west. They must have been an
unnerving sight, for they had only one eye and one tooth between them,
and passed each from one to another when it was required. They refuse to
tell Perseus the whereabouts of their strange sisters and he is forced to steal
their only eye while it is in transit, and hold it to ransom until he obtains
the necessary information.

In this frame, Burne-Jones has included a sort of short-hand précis of the
story in Latin, which effectively cuts down the area he has to work with.
In the low wide space he describes the rocky barrenness of the Graiae's
uncomfortable surroundings, not far from where the earth and the sky meet.
The figures crouch, their hands groping unsuccessfully, trying to retrieve
their lost power of vision. He has clothed the figures in the rippling thin
draperies, reminiscent of dampened cheesecloth, of which other Victorian
Classicists, like Albert Moore and Lord Leighton, were so fond, and which
derive from the type of costume worn by the goddesses of the Parthenon
Pediment, now in the British Museum.

TRANSLATION

*(1) Pallas Athene with her urging spurred Perseus to action and equipped him with
arms. (2) The blind sisters of the Gorgons revealed to him the remote home of the
nymphs. (3) From there he went with wings on his feet and with his head shrouded in
darkness, and (4 & 5) with his sword he struck the one Gorgon who was subject to
death — the others were immortal. (6) Her two sisters arose and pursued him. (7)
Next he turned Atlas to stone, (8 & 9) the sea serpent was slain and Andromeda res-
cued and the comrades of Phineus became lumps of rock. (10) Then Andromeda
looked with wonder in a mirror at the dreadful Medusa.*

PERSEA · CONSILIO · PALLAS · MOVET · INSTRVIT · ARMIS ·
LVMINE · PRIVATAE · MONSTRANT · PENETRALIA · GRAIAE ·
NYMPHARVM · HINC · ALES · PLANTAS · CAPVT · OBDITVS · VMBRIS ·
GORGONA · MORTALEM · DE · NON · MORTALIBVS · VNAM ·
ENSE · FERIT · GEMINAE · SVRGVNT · VRGENTQVE · SORORES ·
SAXEVS · EN · ATLAS · CAESOQVE · EREPTA · DRACONE ·
ANDROMEDA · ET · COMITES · IAM · SAXEA · CORPORA · PHINEI ·
EN · VIRGO · HORRENDAM · IN · SPECVLO · MIRATA · MEDVSAM ·

3

PERSEUS AND THE SEA NYMPHS

Perseus also visited three benign nymphs whose identity varies.
The order of these visits varies too, many commentators placing this visit
before that to the Graiae who live nearer to the Gorgons than to the other
nymphs. The journey is a long and hazardous one and would be difficult to
make without the gifts given to Perseus by the helpful nymphs shown here.
It seems unlikely that Perseus would walk to the end of the earth, near the
Gorgons' abode, find out from the Graiae how to negotiate the last bit of
the journey and then walk all the way back to pick up his borrowed winged
sandals and helmet. Sometimes they are the Stygian Nymphs who inhabit
the region between the Underworld and the land of the living humans.
In either case they are the guardians of a Kibisis, a magic wallet to contain
the Gorgon's head, Hades' helmet of invisibility, and Hermes' handy
winged sandals, all of which are loaned to Perseus through the intercession
of his patroness Athena.

The landscape is as barren as that in which the Graiae live emphasising the
nymphs' remoteness from the world of men, but the lighter tones suggest
an atmosphere of calm quite different from the tension of the preceding
scene. Their disproportionate height and languid pose enhances their
elegance just as contemporary fashion designers elongate the figures of their
drawings in a quite unnatural way for a supposedly elegant effect.

4
THE FINDING OF MEDUSA

At last Perseus arrives in the land of the Gorgons, the land of the setting sun at the western extremity of the world. He locates Medusa, the only mortal one of the sisters, in his mirror as she stands on the left, raising her hands in a vain attempt at self protection, while her sisters crouch under their wings, only recently roused from sleep.

This is the least finished of the series, the positions of the figures only tentatively mapped in, the background an unclear suggestion with little indication of colour. The drama of the scene, however, is conveyed by the starkly contrasting light and shade, dabs of white picking out significant details from the indefinite darkness.

5

THE DEATH OF MEDUSA I

Unknown to Perseus, Medusa is pregnant with the children of Poseidon and when her head is severed, these children, the winged horse Pegasus, later to be tamed and ridden by Bellerophon, and Chrysaor, whose son's cattle were to provide Hercules with his tenth labour, spring fully grown from her neck. The act which resulted in this pregnancy took place inside a temple of Athena and this desecration of a place sacred to her is what engendered Athena's hatred for Medusa in the first place. In the light of this revelation it can be seen that Athena is not merely being altruistic in helping Perseus — as perhaps we thought at the beginning of the story — it happens that by helping him achieve his objective she can also use him as the instrument of her revenge.

In contrast to Number 4, this is a highly finished tightly composed drawing. Severed snakes from Medusa's head drop wriggling to the floor alongside the limp headless body. The space in the picture is shallow, sealed off at the back by a flat backcloth of pink and gold which pushes the figures out at us. Pegasus is drawn with meticulous attention to anatomy and his wings are gilded, as befits such a remarkable beast, but Chrysaor is shown without the curved golden sword from which he derives his name.

6
THE DEATH OF MEDUSA II

Here the other Gorgons, fully awake now and aware of the disaster which has overtaken their sister, make a desperate attempt to follow and attack Perseus, but, aided by Hades' helmet of invisibility and Hermes' sandals, the hero disappears in the darkening clouds, placing the head into the Kibisis, for safety, and so as not to turn everything he passes into stone.

Here Burne-Jones has filled the top three-quarters of his picture with the three massive flying figures, the two startled sisters, spreading their wings on the left and Perseus making a hasty getaway behind the clouds rolling in from the bay. If we look at the brown edge at the bottom of the picture we can see evidence of the method used by the artist to transfer details from smaller preparatory sketches to these large-scale cartoons (drawings the same size as the finished painting). Squares would be drawn on top of the small drawing, and similar squares would be drawn on the blank paper prepared for the cartoon, so that when the main lines of the sketch are transferred the scale of the drawing is preserved.

7

ATLAS TURNED TO STONE

As we mentioned at the beginning, myths are stories invented to explain the natural world. For the Greeks there had to be a reasonable explanation of how the sky was prevented from falling down and crushing the people of the earth. If the sky did not fall down, something somewhere must prop it up. Looking around them, the highest things known to the Greeks and their fellow inhabitants of the Mediterranean were the Atlas Mountains in North Africa, which were so high they disappeared into the sky they supported. That answers one question, but asks another: how did the mountains get there? Mountains are made of rock and stone, how did so much stone come to be piled up to such a great height? The story of Atlas tells us, Atlas was a Titan, a race of giant near-deities of a pre-Zeus generation which was defeated by Zeus and his supporters. As a punishment Atlas was condemned to stand on the earth forever holding up the sky — we can see several signs of the Zodiac in the grey sphere resting on the giant's shoulders. When Perseus flew past, Atlas, who from his great height had seen the whole story, asked that he might be turned to stone and released from his misery and boredom (other stories tell of Atlas' lack of hospitality to the tired Perseus, for which he was petrified by Medusa's head).

The picture shows us the moment at which the giant is turned into stone, transformed into the mountain range which bears his name and supports the sky. Inevitably, nowadays, and particularly for children, this episode is reminiscent of the heroes of American comic-books, but not simply because Atlas is green like the Incredible Hulk. The receding figure of Perseus, flying off in not too confident foreshortening, is not unlike those bulging contemporary heroes Superman and Batman; he even has super-powers and unassailable moral code to match.

8
THE ROCK OF DOOM

To appease the god Poseidon, who had been insulted by the pride of his
wife Cassiopeia, Cepheus, King of Joppa in Ethiopia, had been advised to
sacrifice his daughter, Andromeda, to a sea monster sent by Poseidon to
eat her. Perseus sees the beautiful girl chained to the rocky coast, falls
instantly in love with her and resolves to save her from the monster.

Here we see Perseus removing Hades' helmet so that Andromeda might see
him pausing in flight at the sight of such a beautiful but unusual discovery.
Andromeda stands in a pose which seems remarkably relaxed for one in
such dire circumstances, her head bent demurely as if to emphasise her
shame at her nakedness, which is nevertheless as idealised,
white and chaste, as a marble statue.

9

THE DOOM FULFILLED

Having freed Andromeda from her chains, Perseus used her as bait for the monster rather than simply flying away with her; this would bring the wrath of Poseidon down on the innocent people of the city, and since Perseus is an honourable man he feels this should be prevented. He lay in wait until the seas parted and the huge eel-like creature appeared to claim his tribute, then he emerged from his hiding-place and battled with the monster until it eventually fell dead into the water. At this point we might wonder why Perseus does not simply show the monster Medusa's head and defeat it without risk to himself. We can only conclude that he wanted to show his new girlfriend how brave and strong he was, and how much he loved her — he was showing off.

On the left we are treated to a back view of Andromeda's graceful figure, whose pose seems as unrelated to her danger as her expression.
The rest of the space is given over to the violent struggle between the hero and the monster, whose body coils in sweeping arcs round Perseus to squeeze the life out of him.

1 0

THE BALEFUL HEAD

The final picture in the series shows Perseus and Andromeda together in safety in a luxurious garden. This is presumably after their marriage — undertaken not without a certain amount of opposition from former suitors and the girl's parents — when Perseus has the time and energy to tell his story and to display to his wife the prize he has won. Still, of course, the head may not be looked at directly, and Andromeda may view it only in the safe reflection of a well's calm.

The space in the foreground is emphasised by the foreshortening of the octagonal top of the well and enclosed by the screen of foliage behind the figures. The surface of the picture is highly finished and details are carefully noted, but the picture is balanced and quiet as befits its subject matter, no wind disturbs the water or shakes the leaves from the trees, just as no disturbances remain to interrupt the couple's happiness.

This is where Burne-Jones ends the series. His ten panels are complete, none of the episodes illustrated could have been omitted without disturbing the flow of the narrative, but the story does not end here. It hinges on Perseus' desire for revenge upon the evil Polydectes and is not complete until this revenge is obtained. Returning to Seriphos, Perseus found that his mother and Diktys had taken refuge in a temple to escape from the King. He went straight to the palace where he found Polydectes feasting self-indulgently (some say that the feast is the same as the one in progress when Perseus departed). He proclaimed his return, announced his gift and, when mocked in disbelief, produced the dreadful head from his magic sack, averted his eyes and turned the revellers and their king into a circle of stones which may still be seen on the island.

Properly avenged at last, he returned his borrowed weapons to the Sea Nymphs, gave the head of Medusa to Athena, who wore it from then on as part of her insignia and, placing Diktys on the throne of Seríphos, set off for Argos. His grandfather fled, fearing the consequences of Perseus' return and the hero became King in his place. Sometime later, while competing in a series of competitive games, Perseus threw a discus into the crowd of spectators, wounding an old man on the foot. On examination, the old man proved to be none other than his grandfather, Acrisius, and despite its position, the injury turned out to be fatal, thus fulfilling the prophecy made at the Delphic Oracle at the beginning of the story.

Deeply saddened by this occurrence, Perseus left Argos, but taking Andromeda with him, he founded, according to one tradition, the Greek city of Mycenae and a great dynasty from which kings of Persia claimed descent and through which they asserted their rights to the kingdoms of Greece.

The stories of Perseus' death are indistinct and conflicting. Eventually, however, Perseus and Andromeda were placed in the heavens as constellations through the influence of the goddess Athena, presumably in recognition of services rendered, and there they remain undisturbed.

If you would like to read the full story of Perseus, and the other characters mentioned briefly here, you might refer to *The Heroes* by Charles Kingsley, or for a fully annotated version, *The Greek Myths* by Robert Graves.

MICHAEL CASSIN

The Perseus Story
Sir Edward Coley Burne-Jones, Tate Gallery, London

The Baring Room, Southampton City Art Gallery
© Joe Low

THE
PERSEUS
SERIES

The Perseus Series was commissioned in 1875 by Lord Arthur Balfour, later to become the British Prime Minister in 1885. Lord Balfour was a leading figure in the 'Souls', which was a group of like-minded intellectual aristocrats who were admirers of artistic sensibility. Burne-Jones and Balfour became friends after being introduced by the Countess of Airlie in the Spring of 1875 and Balfour developed into a dedicated patron of his art. He had previously acquired another work by Burne-Jones, *The Wheel of Fortune*, and he intended *The Perseus Series* to hang in the music room of his London home at 4 Carlton Gardens. Burne-Jones and Lord Balfour agreed on the subject from an earlier treatment of the legend 'The Doom of King Acrisius' from William Morris' book *The Earthly Paradise*. The book contained many versions of Greek myths and fairytales, Burne-Jones illustrated the book for his colleague, which was to enthuse him to paint many illustrations on a larger scale. The choice of the story of Perseus gave Burne-Jones the opportunity to depict his most favoured themes, the conquest of good over evil and the triumph of beauty, both encapsulated in a narrative content.

On 27 March 1875 Burne-Jones visited Carlton Gardens to survey the site intended for his paintings. He decided that the lighting in the music room was too harsh, all the windows had to be re-glazed and the walls re-panelled with light English oak. He designed the paintings to hang in a band around the room, with *The Death of Medusa I* above the doorway. Burne-Jones instructed continuing 'resembling the procession by Mantegna at Hampton Court'. He told Balfour that an oak ceiling must also be added to the room and that it should be lit by candlelight. It is very interesting to see how Burne-Jones designed not only the paintings but also the surrounding in which he wanted them to be displayed. Burne-Jones made detailed drawings of the exact position he wished the works to be placed (see p. 41), and he intended William Morris, his lifetime friend, to create old English patterns around each painting, rather like a carved-wood border.

The preliminary studies of the paintings show how Burne-Jones simplified the events of the myth into a single action, each painting representing a significant occurrence in the narrative. One can see the development between the preliminary sketches and the full-scale cartoons though there are changes to the content of several paintings. Lord Balfour visited Burne-Jones at his home, The Grange, and approved the sketches. He then put into place the expensive alterations recommended by Burne-Jones and the artist began work on the full-scale cartoons.

The cartoon studies for the finished paintings were drawn to scale and then finished in gouache. They were specifically produced to allow the artist to find the correct dimensions and perspective. Burne-Jones worked on the ten cartoon panels until 1885, then began to recreate them on canvas. Sadly the series of oils was never completed due to Burne-Jones' worsening health and mental fatigue. The unfinished series of oil paintings are now in the Staatsgalerie, Stuttgart, Germany (see p. 50 for details of work).

Each of the ten cartoons are a testimony to the definitive style of Burne-Jones, in particular the distinctive way in which he portrayed the female nude. In the painting, *The Rock of Doom*, one senses the characteristic peace that the artist brings to his work.

In the narrative, Andromeda is awaiting death, as she is sacrificed to a sea monster, her pose is lifeless, her expression vacant and she seems absolutely unaware of the terror which is about to behold her. One explanation for this particular calm may be due to the length of time the artist often spent working on each painting, some taking over ten years from conception to realisation. Burne-Jones was always concerned with the enchantment of his figures, he was fascinated with their grace to the point of making them lifeless, *The Perseus Series* substantiates this trait exceptionally well.

The impact of his Italian tour in 1873 where he encountered the masterpieces of Michelangelo is also evident in *The Perseus Series*, particularly in his depiction of the male nude. This is accentuated further by the influence of the over-developed forms of classical Greek and Roman art, which were in vogue during Burne-Jones' lifetime.

The Perseus Series cartoons are a unique and treasured part of Southampton City Art Gallery's outstanding collection (see p. 49 for the history of the series). As the finished series of paintings was never completed, Lord Balfour never had the opportunity to see the artist's work finally realised in his music room. However, *The Perseus Series* cartoons today hang in a room similar to that which Burne-Jones originally intended. This room is unique from the rest of the other galleries, rather than pristine white walls, it has rich, dark mahogany panels incorporating a large marble fireplace. The wall panels, doors and fireplace all originate from the boardroom of the merchant bankers, Baring Brothers and Company Ltd. In 1913 the headquarters of Baring Brothers were erected under the supervision of the famous Edwardian architect, Gerald Horseley F.R.I.B.A. at No 8 Bishopsgate, London. In 1975 the bank's headquarters were demolished to make way for new roads and in the spirit of European Architectural Heritage Year, Baring Brothers presented the boardroom fittings to Southampton City Council. The fittings of the Baring Room were carefully reassembled by a team of highly skilled craftsmen from Vosper Thornycroft, members of the Union of Construction, Allied Trades and Technicians to create a beautiful new setting in the City Art Gallery. This room made an ideal backdrop for *The Perseus Series* and so, in late 1975, the works were installed and have been displayed there until 1998-9 when they travel to New York, Birmingham and Paris taking pride of place in the celebrated Burne-Jones centenary exhibition.

ESTA JONES

SOUTHAMPTON CITY ART GALLERY

BURNE-JONES
CHRONOLGY

Born 28 August 1833 in central Birmingham. Mother dies six days after his birth.

1852   Goes to Exeter College, Oxford, where he meets William Morris (1834-1896), his life-long friend.

1855   Trip to France with Morris to see Medieval Cathedrals. Decides to pursue a career as an artist.

1856   Becomes the pupil of Dante Gabriel Rossetti. Morris and Burne-Jones share a studio at 17, Red Lion Square, London, which they decorate with medieval style furniture.

1857   With Rossetti, Morris, Arthur Hughes, Val Prinsep, Spencer Stanhope and J. Hungerford Pollen paints the Oxford Union Murals.

1858   Founding of the Hogarth Club, an exhibiting society made up of the artists in Rossetti's circle.

1859   First trip to Northern Italy.

1860   Red House built for Morris and his new bride, Jane. Burne-Jones marries Georgiana Macdonald.

1861   Founding of the Firm: Morris, Marshall, Faulkner and Co.

1862   Trip to Italy with his wife and John Ruskin.

1864   Public debut at the Royal Water-Colour Society: *The Merciful Knight* and *The Annunciation*.

1864-66 *St. George Series* for Myles Birket Foster.

1867   Moves into The Grange, Fulham.

1868-1871   Involvement with Maria Zambaco.

1870   Resigns from the Royal Water-Colour Society after being accused of creating an indecent work in *Phyllis and Demophoon*.

1871 and 1873   Trips to Italy: impact of the art of Michelangelo and Piero della Francesca.

1875   *The Perseus Series* for Lord Arthur Balfour begun.

1877   Opening of the Grosvenor Gallery. Burne-Jones achieves public acclaim.

1880   *The Golden Stairs* for Lord Battersea.

1884   *King Cophetua and the Beggar Maid* for Lord Wharncliffe.

1870-1890 *The Briar Rose Series* purchased by Lord Faringdon.

1898   On the 16 June Burne-Jones dies and is buried at Rottingdean. His memorial service on 23 June was the first ever held in Westminster Abbey in honour of a painter.

LIST OF WORKS

Inv. no 100   *The Call of Perseus*   1525 x 1270 mm (60 x 50 ins)

Inv. no 101   *Perseus and the Graiae*   1525 x 1705 mm (60 x 67⅛ ins)

Inv. no 102   *Perseus and the Sea Nymphs*   1528 x 1264 mm (60 x 49¾ ins)

Inv. no 103   *The Finding of Medusa*   1525 x 1377 mm (60 x 54¼ ins)

Inv. no 109   *The Death of Medusa I*   1245 x 1169 mm (49 x 46 ins)

Inv. no 104   *The Death of Medusa II*   1525 x 1365 mm (60 x 53¾ ins)

Inv. no 105   *Atlas Turned to Stone*   1525 x 1900 mm (60 x 74¾ ins)

Inv. no 107   *The Rock of Doom*   1540 x 1286 mm (60⅝ x 50⅝ ins)

Inv. no 106   *The Doom Fulfilled*   1538 x 1384 mm (60½ x 54½ ins)

Inv. no 108   *The Baleful Head*   1537 x 1290 mm (60½ x 50¾ ins)

All works are gouache on paper laid on linen canvas

PROVENANCE

Alexander Henderson, later first Lord Faringdon, by whom purchased from the artist; Lady Violet Henderson, from whom purchased by Southampton City Art Gallery for £3,500 for the series of ten, December 1934 (Chipperfield Bequest Fund, advisor Sir Kenneth Clark, Director, National Gallery, London).

NOTES

Perseus: The model for Perseus was a gypsy named Smith (see Harrison & Waters, 1973 p. 119).

102 *Perseus and the Sea Nymphs*: The nymph on the right was modelled on Frances Horner (née Graham, see Harrison & Waters, 1973, p. 113). Sketches of Frances Graham by Burne-Jones were sold through Christies, London, on 5 November 1993 (lot 120, 371 x 273 mm) and 10 March 1995 (lot 156, 597 x 445 mm). The Arts Council of Great Britain (ACGB) catalogue 1975 (p . 59) cites Dr Löcher's comparison of the pose of Perseus to the 'ignudi' of the Sistine Chapel ceiling which Burne-Jones studied on his visit to Rome in 1871.

103 *The Finding of Medusa*: Mrs Drummond, the sister of W.A.S. Benson was the model for Medusa (see Harrison and Waters, 1973, p. 113 and Fitzgerald, 1975, p. 172).

106/107 *The Doom Fulfilled* and *The Rock of Doom*: The original version of these designs incorporated both works in one panel with metal sheets finished off with paint to represent the armour but this experimental technique was abandoned after strong criticism on the oil painting's first showing at the Grosvenor Gallery (see Harrison & Waters, 1973, p. 120 and Fitzgerald, 1975, p. 204).

108 *The Baleful Head*: see Treuherz (1984, p. 167) who notes Burne-Jones' admiration for the illuminations of a 15th century 'Roman de Rose' manuscript in the collection of the British Museum, London. The reflection in the well is a Narcissus miniature being adapted to form the central motif of *The Baleful Head* composition.

109 *The Death of Medusa I*: see Kestner, 1984, pp. 113-4 for an interpretation of this work as a product of sexual repression.

SOME RELATED WORKS

The finished oil paintings are in the Staatsgalerie, Stuttgart, Germany:

Inv. no 3103 *The Call of Perseus* *
(Die Berufung des Perseus) 1527 x 1270 mm (60⅛ x 50 ins)

Inv. no 3105 *Perseus and the Graiae*
(Perseus und die Graien) 1535 x 1700 mm (60½ x 67 ins)

Inv. no 3104 *Perseus and the Sea Nymphs* *
(Perseus und die Meernymphen) 1530 x 1270 mm (60¼ x 50 ins)

Inv. no 3108 *The Rock of Doom*
(Der Schicksalsfelsen) 1550 x 1300 mm (61 x 51¼ ins)

Inv. no 3109 *The Doom Fulfilled*
(Die Erfullung des Schicksals) 1550 x 1405 mm (61 x 55⅜ ins)

Inv. no 3110 *The Baleful Head*
(Das Schreckenshaupt) 1550 x 1300 mm (61 x 51¼ ins)

* These two oil paintings in the Staatsgalerie, Stuttgart of *The Call of Perseus* and *Perseus and the Sea Nymphs* were never completed. They were worked on in 1897 and are very different in style, see Kurt Löcher *Der Perseus-Zyklus von Edward Burne-Jones*, Stuttgart, 1973 and the ACGB exhibition catalogue, 1975, nos 159 and 162.

The four completed oil paintings from the Staatsgalerie were exhibited in England in 1975 by the Arts Council of Great Britain, inv. no 3105 *Perseus and the Graiae* cat. no 161; inv. no 3108 *The Rock of Doom* cat. no 169; inv. no 3109 *The Doom Fulfilled* cat. no 171; inv. no 3110 *The Baleful Head* cat. no 173.

There are also two sketches for *The Perseus Series* in the Staatsgalerie, Stuttgart.

Inv. no 3106 *The Finding of Medusa* (Die Auffingdung de Medusa) 1520 x 1370 mm (59⅞ x 54 ins)

Inv. no 3107 *The Death of Medusa* (Der Tod der Medusa) 1520 x 1370 mm (59⅞ x 54 ins)

The original designs for *The Story of Perseus* by Edward Burne-Jones: Tate Gallery London, collection, *The Call of Perseus, Perseus and the Graiae and the Neirids* (1875-6) which relates to Southampton's 100, 101, 102 (Tate inv. no 3456); *The Finding of Medusa; The Death of Medusa (The Birth of Pegasus and Chrysaor) and Perseus Pursued by the Gorgons* (1875-6) which relates to Southampton's 103, 109, 104 (Tate inv. no 3457); *Atlas Turned to Stone, The Rock of Doom and The Doom Fulfilled; The Court of Phineas and The Baleful Head* (1875-6) which relates to Southampton's 105, 107 and 108 (Tate inv. no 3458). Presented to the Tate by the Trustees of the Chantry Bequest in 1919, see *The Age of Rossetti, Burne-Jones and Watts — Symbolism in Britain 1860-1910*, Tate Gallery exhibition catalogue 1997, cat. nos 93, 94 and 95, pp. 227-8.

The Finding of Medusa: 'Studies of Armour', watercolour on paper, V&A collection, see *Sir Edward Burne-Jones* (catalogue), Fulham Library, London, 1967, p. 8.

The Death of Medusa I: 'Chrysaor', water-colour and gold paint on brown paper, Fulham Library collection, see *Sir Edward Burne-Jones* (catalogue), Fulham Library, London 1967, p. 8.

*The Rock of Doom: 'Perseus and Andromeda' c.*1876, The Art Gallery of South Australia, Adelaide, an early version of the work in which 107 *The Rock of Doom* and 106 *The Doom Fulfilled* are combined in one panel (see Löcher, Stuttgart, 1973, no 8c, p. 90).

The Doom Fulfilled: 'Studies of Armour', water-colour and silver paint on brown paper, V&A collection, see 'The Decorative Art of Sir Edward Burne-Jones, Baronet' by Valliance, Aymer in the Easter number of *The Art Journal*, London, 1900, p. 26, fig. 46 and *Sir Edward Burne-Jones* (catalogue), Fulham Library, London, 1967, p. 7.

The Baleful Head: 'Studies of Armour', water-colour on brown paper, V&A collection, see *Sir Edward Burne-Jones* (catalogue), Fulham Library, London, 1967, p. 8.

Study for the Head of Perseus in The Arming of Perseus, 1875, pencil, British Museum collection (1967-10-14-49), see ACGB catalogue, 1975, cat. no 163.

Study for Perseus in The Finding of Medusa, Fitzwilliam Museum, Cambridge (679), see ACGB catalogue, 1975, cat. no 165. Also an inferior version (dated 1881) in Birmingham.

Two studies for Medusa in The Finding of Medusa, Lady Lever Art Gallery, Port Sunlight, see ACGB exhibition catalogue, 1975, cat. no 166.

Two studies of wings for The Death of Medusa, both 1882, pencil, Manchester City Art Gallery, (1925, 137a-b), see ACGB catalogue, 1975, cat. no 168.

*Two studies of a helmet, c.*1885, coloured chalk on grey/brown paper, Witt Collection, Courtauld Institute of Art, London, see ACGB catalogue, 1975, cat. no 170.

Study for Andromeda in The Doom Fulfilled, 1885, pencil, British Museum collection (1967-10-14-48), see ACGB catalogue 1975, cat. no 172.

*Study for The Baleful Head, c.*1885, pencil, Fitzwilliam Museum, Cambridge, see ACGB catalogue, 1975, cat. no 174.

Sketchbook 1886-1889, 146 pages, pencil and crayons, leather bound, V&A collection (E.9-1955), see ACGB catalogue, 1975, cat. no 175, contains early ideas for a number of works Burne-Jones was working on at the time, including *The Rock of Doom* and *The Baleful Head*.

Sketchbook, July 1875, pencil, linen board bound, Birmingham Museums and Art Gallery collection (P.5-25), see ACGB catalogue, 1975, cat. no 176, contains a series of sketches for *The Perseus Series* soon after Burne-Jones received the commission.

Nude Study for The Call of Perseus, chalk on brown paper, *c.*1887, collection of Mrs Robert Beloe in 1976, see ACGB catalogue, 1975, cat. no 160.

Perseus and the Graiae, small oil, UK private collection in 1976, see ACGB catalogue, 1975, cat. no 161.

Nude Study for Perseus in The Call of Perseus, collection of Mrs David Daniels, New York, USA in 1976, see ACGB catalogue, 1975, cat. no 160.

EXHIBITION HISTORY

The Pre-Raphaelites, Whitechapel Art Gallery, London, 8 April – 12 May 1948. *The Call of Perseus* cat. no 12; *Perseus and the Graiae* cat. no 13; *Perseus and the Sea Nymphs* cat. no 24 (titled *The Arming of Perseus*); *The Finding of Medusa* cat. no 14; *The Death of Medusa I* cat. no 20; *The Death of Medusa II* cat. no 15; *Atlas Turned to Stone* cat. no 16; *The Rock of Doom* cat. no 18; *The Doom Fulfilled* cat. no 17; *The Baleful Head* cat. no 19.

Ten Decades of British Taste, R.B.A (Royal Society of British Artists) Galleries, The Institute of Contemporary Arts (I.C.A.), London, 10 August – 27 September 1951. *The Finding of Medusa* cat. no 117; *The Death of Medusa II* cat. no 118.

Nineteenth-Century Paintings and Drawings from the Permanent Collection, Southampton Art Gallery, 1 November 1958- 4 January 1959. *The Call of Perseus* cat. no 33; *Perseus and the Graiae* cat. no 34; *Perseus and the Sea Nymphs* cat. no 35 (titled *Perseus in the Garden of the Nymphs*); *The Finding of Medusa* cat. no 36 (titled *Perseus About to Sever the Head of Medusa*); *The Death of Medusa I* cat. no 42 (titled *The Birth of Pegasus and Chrysaor from the Blood of Medusa*); *The Death of Medusa II* cat. no 37 (titled *The Escape of Perseus*); *Atlas Turned to Stone* cat. no 33; *The Rock of Doom* cat. no 40 (titled *The Rescue of Andromeda*); *The Doom Fulfilled* cat. no 39 (titled *Perseus Slaying the Serpent*); *The Baleful Head* cat. no 41 (titled *Perseus and his Bride*).

The Nude in Victorian Art, Harrogate City Art Gallery 6-30 August 1966. *The Call of Perseus* cat. no 55; *The Death of Medusa II* cat. no 57; *The Doom Fulfilled* cat. no 56.

Burne-Jones, The Mappin Art Gallery, Sheffield, 23 October – 28 November 1971. *The Call of Perseus* cat. no 132; *Perseus and the Graiae* cat. no 133; *Perseus and the Sea Nymphs* cat. no 134 (titled *In the Garden of the Nymphs*); *The Finding of Medusa* cat. no 135; *The Death of Medusa I* cat. no 141 (titled *The Birth of Pegasus*); *The Death of Medusa II* cat. no 136 (titled *The Escape of Perseus*); *Atlas Turned to Stone* cat. no 137; *The Rock of Doom* cat. no 139 (titled *The Rescue of Andromeda*); *The Doom Fulfilled* cat. no 138 (titled *Perseus Slaying the Serpent*); *The Baleful Head* cat. no 140 (titled *Perseus and his Bride*).

Burne-Jones: The Paintings, Graphic and Decorative Work of Sir Edward Burne-Jones 1833-1898, Arts Council of Great Britain, London, 5 November 1975 – 3 April 1976 (touring The Hayward Gallery, London, Southampton Art Gallery and Birmingham Museums and Art Gallery). *The Call of Perseus* cat. no 159; *Perseus and the Sea Nymphs* cat. no 162 (titled *The Arming of Perseus*); *The Finding of Medusa* cat. no 164; *The Death of Medusa II* cat. no 167.

Le Symbolisme en Europe, Museum Boijmans, Rotterdam (touring Brussels, Baden-Baden and Paris) 14 November 1975 – 19 July 1976. *Atlas Turned to Stone* cat. no 19; *The Baleful Head* cat. no 20.

Pre-Raphaelite Paintings, Lowe Art Museum, University of Miami, U.S.A., March 1972. *The Doom Fulfilled.*

Sir Edward Coley Burne-Jones Centenary Exhibition, The Metropolitan Museum of Art, New York, U.S.A., 1 June – 6 November 1998 (touring Birmingham Museums and Art Gallery, U.K., 17 October – 17 January 1999 and Musée d'Orsay, Paris, 1 March - 6 June 1999). The complete *Perseus Series* loaned, catalogue numbers not available at time of going to press.

LITERATURE

The above exhibition catalogues and in addition:

Bell, Malcolm *Sir Edward Burne-Jones A Record and Review*, London, 4th edition 1898, *The Call of Perseus* p. 58 (repro); *The Baleful Head* (repro).

Cecil, David *Visionary and Dreamer*, London, 1969, *The Doom Fulfilled*.

Fitzgerald, Penelope *Edward Burne-Jones: A Biography*, London, 1975, *Perseus and the Graiae* p. 24; *The Finding of Medusa* p. 24.

Harrison, Martin & Waters, Bill *Burne-Jones*, London, 1973, *The Call of Perseus* page 119; *Perseus and the Graiae* p. 120; *Perseus and the Sea Nymphs* p. 113; *The Finding of Medusa* page 112; *The Death of Medusa I* p. 119 (repro b&w); *The Death of Medusa II*.

Ironside, Robin & Gere, John *Pre-Raphaelite Painters*, London, 1948, *The Call of Perseus* p. (repro); *Perseus and the Sea Nymphs*.

Johnson, May *Burne-Jones: All Colour Paperback*, London, 1979

Kestner, J 'Burne-Jones and Nineteenth-Century Misogyny' in *Biography: An Interdisciplinary Quarterly*, 1984, *The Death of Medusa* p. 109; *The Rock of Doom* pp. 111-2; *The Doom Fulfilled* pp. 111-4; *The Baleful Head* pp. 115-6.

Lewis, Wyndham Review in *The Listener*, 22 April 1948, *The Death of Medusa II*.

Lisle, Fortunée de *Burne-Jones*, London, 1904, *The Call of Perseus* p. 130; *Perseus and the Sea Nymphs* p. 131; *The Finding of Medusa* p. 131.

Löcher, Kurt 'Der Perseus-Zyklus von Edward Burne-Jones, Stuttgart, 1973, *The Call of Perseus* (no 1d) b&w repro p. 25; *Perseus and the Graiae* (no 2d) b&w repro p. 36; *Perseus and the Sea Nymphs* (no 3e) b&w repro p. 43; *The Finding of Medusa* (no 4e) b&w repro p. 56; *The Death of Medusa I* (no 5c) repro p. 66; *The Death of Medusa II* (no 6f) b&w repro p. 72; *Atlas Turned to Stone* (no 7d) b&w repro p. 86; *The Rock of Doom* (no 8p) b&w repro p. 91; *The Doom Fulfilled* (no 9h) b&w repro p. 103; *The Baleful Head* (no 11s) b&w repro p. 136.

Moffatt, James 'Mr Balfour as a Man of Letters' in *The Bookman*, London, August 1912, pp. 193-201 (photographs of some of the original oil paintings, now in Stuttgart, in Mr Balfour's home).

Rose, Andrea 'The Pre-Raphaelites', Oxford, 1977.

Treuherz, Julian 'The Pre-Raphaelites and Mediaeval Manuscripts' in *Pre-Raphaelite Papers*, ed. Leslie Parris, London, 1984, *The Baleful Head*, p. 167.

Research into The Perseus Series *held by Southampton City Art Gallery has not been undertaken in recent years and the above text represents a summary of the information held in the gallery files as of January 1998. Information is presented as it is held in the files and Southampton City Art Gallery apologises for any possible inaccuracies contained in the records as they are reproduced here.*

HELEN SIMPSON

REGISTRAR

SOUTHAMPTON CITY ART GALLERY

CONTRIBUTING AUTHORS
Anne Anderson, F.S.A.
Senior Lecturer, Fine Art Valuation, Southampton Institute.

Michael Cassin, Assistant Keeper of Education at Southampton City Art Gallery, 1979-1981,
Head of Education at the National Galleries of Scotland, 1998.

© Southampton City Art Gallery and authors
March 1998
Edition 5000
Paperback ISBN – 0 901723 18 5
Edited by Stephen Snoddy & Esta Jones
Design and Production by Alan Ward, Axis Design, Manchester
Photography by John Lawrence, Southampton City Art Gallery
Printed by Jackson Wilson, Leeds
Reprographics by Leeds Photo Litho

This book has been set in Mrs Eaves & Mrs Eaves Smart Ligatures from the Emigre Font Library.
The fonts are based on the design Baskerville (John Baskerville, 1706-75, Birmingham, England), and are named after his
live-in housekeeper who later became his wife, Sarah Eaves. She continued printing his unfinished type volumes after his death.

Published on the occasion of the Burne-Jones Centenary Exhibition at
The Metropolitan Museum of Art, New York, 1 June – 6 September 1998
Birmingham Museums and Art Gallery, 17 October 1998 – 17 January 1999
Musée d'Orsay, Paris, 1 March – 6 June 1999

Southampton City Art Gallery
Civic Centre, Southampton, England, SO14 7LP
Telephone +44 (0) 1703 832277
Facsimile +44 (0) 1703 832153

In memory of Cllr. Eddie Read 1947 – 1998
Chair of Leisure 1987 – 1998